Self-Defense for Women

JERROLD N. OFFSTEIN, Third Degree Black Belt
Teaching Specialist, Stanford University

 National Press Books

To Elena

Library of Congress Catalog Card Number: 72-77170
International Standard Book Number: 0-87484-209-3
Manufactured in the United States of America

Book design by Nancy Sears
Photos by Dick Keeble

Contents
(Listing Chapters and Tactics)

Introduction

This book is the direct result of a series of courses in self-defense for women taught both at Stanford University and at our private school since the Spring of 1970. The course had its origin in a conversation between the Stanford Black Belt Society and the Dean of Women's Office at Stanford in 1970. As almost everywhere, the threat to the personal safety of Stanford women had reached a point of requiring more than the traditional warnings on how to avoid sexual assault.

To meet this situation with a more practical set of responses to sexual assault, our approach was to survey the available literature, data, and studies as well as to interview public officials on the subject of rape and assaults on women generally.

From this pool of information we learned certain facts we had not previously known. According to the reports, the most important of these were the following:

1. The typical sexual assault on a woman is committed by someone who knows her, at least by sight, and is afraid of her. His fear is implicit in his choosing this method of "communicating" with the woman! Second, he is fearful that he will be recognized and punished for his attack. This second fear accounts for the fact

that most physical abuse takes place *after* the assault, often to prevent recognition or reporting.
2. Most rapes are not reported, for a variety of reasons, none of which casts much credit on our institutions of protection and our courts.
3. Those rapes perpetrated by "strangers" are generally done in areas that make the person attacked less able to attract assistance.
4. An unprepared woman generally offers little or no resistance to her attacker.
5. An assailant generally uses a limited number of tactics to overpower his victim.

According to our research in *100%* of the cases in which the woman *successfully repelled or escaped from* the assault, there was one common element: *resistance* by the attacked woman; whether it was the making of noise or physical resistance or a combination of the two. *No one* that we could find got free by compliance with the attacker.

From this data, Nobuo Sato (2° black belt, Shotokan Karate), John Hu (2° black belt, Kenpo Karate) and I devised a course of practical self-defense to meet the threat of sexual assault as we saw it from our research and experience in the field. The course consisted of elements, tactics and techniques from Karate, jiu-jitsu, judo and aikido. It was a compendium of skills rather than a presentation of any one of these martial arts alone.

The first course was presented in 1970 at Stanford. After that class we evaluated our experience and student feedback and did the first of the modifications of the course. The process of review and modification has continued, to meet our skills with new knowledge and to meet the needs of our students. Instructors using this system should likewise balance their knowledge and martial arts skills with the experience of other instructors and perceptions of students.

Some students have questions about whether they have the coordination, courage or physical stamina to complete such a course. It has been our extensive experience that women (and men) of all ages (13 to senility), occupations and states of physical condition can complete this course and be able to defend themselves from assaults to the extent of being able to counter and break free from such assaults. We know through our students that the course works. It works *if* the student applies herself to both learning and practicing the methods and tactics of self-defense. How useful the course will be to her will be directly proportionate to the effort she invests in it. In the first part of the text we *briefly* discuss some martial arts, and their psychological and spiritual concepts. The discussion covers only that information that will be useful to *this* course. If you are inclined to investigate the various martial arts further, your library or bookstore will have more on the ones discussed here (and many more). We hold no one to be any "better" than any other. They are merely different from one another.

Approach the class with a serious mind and dedication realizing that you are learning physical "motor skills," and only by *repetition,* in the form of regular *practice,* can you hope to acquire the necessary *competence* to give you the *confidence* to respond to an assault and counter it in order to *escape.*

Your best defense is *distance.* Be alert to dangerous situations and avoid them, if possible. If unable to avoid them, repel the assault with the confidence that comes from the competence you have acquired in this course.

You must use your judgment in deciding *whether* or *how* to resist. In some situations you may be forced to choose between a number of unpleasant alternatives. But choose you must. Remember, *no one,* we found, escaped *sexual assault* by passive resistance; and in the primary data source used, *60%* of all the successfully repelled assaults were accomplished by the presentation of *loud noise alone.* Practice your yell. It is a *very* effective *weapon* for you to have available for your self-defense.

Karate: its history, philosophy and principles

The study of the unarmed combat skills, generically known by the modern Japanese term "Karate," originated as a method of exercise and self-defense based on the effective use of the unarmed body of the practitioner. This system consisted of techniques of blocking or thwarting an attack and counter-attacking the opponent by striking, punching and/or kicking. The modern study of Karate is the result of a more thorough organization and scientific rationalization of its techniques compared to the older system.

There are three branches of the martial arts commonly called Karate; they are (1) as physical education, (2) self-defense and (3) competitive sport. Karate is based on the application of the laws of physics, psychology and anatomy. It is this constant search for opportunities to apply the laws of physical and metaphysical science to movements of the body that distinguishes Karate from other martial arts.

As physical education, Karate is almost without equal. Since it is highly dynamic and makes balanced use of a large number of muscles, it provides excellent all-round exercise and develops coordination and agility. Many college women are enthusiastically studying Karate or some other self-defense system, since beyond its practical defense application lies an excellent moderate exercise system. These arts are widely studied by both children and older people for both physical development and pleasure.

This is *not* a course in Karate. It is an amalgam of many of the martial arts, but since its basis is in Karate forms we will dispel a good deal of misinformation about the martial arts and at the same time discuss elements basic to learning self-defense.

There are many theories and myths regarding the history and development of the martial arts. The best authenticated and most widely accepted explanation of the development of the arts popularly called Karate is an old Chinese legend. This legend recounts that the Indian Buddhist Bonze (monk) Dharuma Taishi journeyed from India to China to instruct a Liang-dynasty monarch in the tenets of Buddhism. To make such a long and arduous journey alone along a route that is still nearly impassible was no mean feat and testifies to Dharuma's powers of physical and mental endurance. He remained in China at a monastery in Southern China called Shao Lin-szu, teaching Buddhism to the monks. Tradition relates how the severe discipline Dharuma imposed and the pace he set caused the student monks to pass out, one-by-one, from sheer physical exhaustion. At the next assembly he explained to them that, although the aim of Buddhism is the salvation of the soul, the body and the soul exist together and in their weakened physical state the monks could never perform the ascetic practices necessary for the attainment of true enlightenment. To remedy the situation he began to teach them a system of physical and mental discipline embodied in the *I-chin Sutra,* an ancient Oriental text on the origins and principles of Karate. As time went on, the monks at Shao Lin-szu formed the basis of Chuan-fa or Kenpo, as it is called in America and Europe.

This system branched out northward and towards Okinawa. In Okinawa the art became known as Okinawa-te or the "Hands of Okinawa." Both there and as the art traveled northward in China it also became a self-defense or fighting style. Some names taken by these variations on the original system were Kung-fu, Shao-lin and Kendo. When the art reached Korea, the first "crushing" or "breaking" blows were developed by the warlord Harondo class to kill an opponent even though he had on body armor. The two main Korean styles are called Tang Soo-Do ("the study of unarmed combat") and Tae Kwon-Do ("the study of Kicks and Punches"). In Japan the art arrived about 1900 and got the name Karate or "empty hands." The custom of the Samurai had been to fight with swords ("sai") or sticks and spears ("bo" and "bokken").

Judo is a Japanese form of wrestling; jiu-jitsu, a system of "miscellaneous" defensive tactics, and

aikido are also defensive systems notable for
their use of pressure points and body joint
manipulation.

THE PRINCIPLES OF KARATE

The remarkable strength manifested by many
Karate techniques, both offensive and defensive,
is not the mysterious, esoteric thing many ob-
servers, as well as some practitioners of the art
itself, would have one believe. On the contrary, it
is the inevitable result of the effective application
of several well-known scientific principles to the
movements of the body. Likewise, knowledge of
psychological principles, along with constant
practice, enable the student to find proper open-
ings and execute the proper tactic at the right
time. At an advanced level it is possible for one
to anticipate the movements of the opponent.

Before learning the various individual techniques,
it is necessary to have a clear understanding of
the physical, psychological and the physical-psy-
chological principles which underlie them all. Of
course, it is most difficult to interpret complex
physical or psychological processes in terms of a
few simple principles. Likewise, mastery of these
principles will come only after arduous practice.

Physical Principles

Maximum Strength: Any movement of the body
depends on muscular expansion and contraction.
There are many factors involved in exerting maximum force through control of these expansions

and contractions, and only the most basic of these are discussed here.

1. Force is directly proportionate to the degree of muscular expansion and contraction. This is the principle behind, for example, the coil spring—the more the spring is compressed the greater force it exerts when released. Muscles react in a very similar fashion.

2. The striking power of a force is inversely proportionate to the time required for its delivery. This means that in Karate *it is not the muscular strength used to lift a heavy object that is required,* but the *strength manifested in terms of speed of muscular expansion and contraction.* In other words force is *accumulated* in the form of *speed,* and at the end of the movement, speed is converted into *striking force.* In standard scientific terminology force equals mass times the square of the velocity.

Concentration of Strength: To perform any kind of strenuous work concentration of strength is required. Even a great amount of strength will accomplish little if it is dispersed. By the same token, a small amount of strength, properly concentrated, can be quite powerful. It is no exaggeration to say that the concentration of strength at the proper time and in the proper place is far more effective in self-defense than a greater amount of unfocused brute strength. The following principles are basic:

1. Other things being equal, the shorter the time a force is in transit from point of delivery to point of striking, the more effective it is. This element of concentration of strength is very

important to you in learning to defend yourself from attack because it allows you to move immediately into the next technique you will use in your defense, whatever it might be.

2. The greater the number of muscles brought into play in performing a given movement, the greater the concentration of strength. By this principle strength is concentrated at the point of impact.

3. Maximum concentration of bodily strength depends on effective utilization of the forces produced by exertion of the various muscles. When the muscles are properly coordinated the resultant force is greater; when they are *not* so coordinated, it is lessened.

4. Concentration of strength depends *not* on simultaneous exertion of all the body's muscles, but on their exertion in the proper order. The muscles of the abdominal and pelvic regions are powerful, but slow, whereas those of the extremities are fast but weak. In order to concentrate the force of both sets of muscles, those of the abdomen and hips must be brought into play first, and this force transferred to the point of impact by either the hands or the feet.

Utilizing Reaction Force: This refers to the well known principle of physics: to every action there is an opposite, and equal, reaction. This principle finds wide use in this self-defense course: for example, in punching out with the hand, the *other* hand is simultaneously withdrawn to the hips, adding reaction-force to the punching hand.

Running or jumping is made possible by pressing

downward with the opposite foot. This is an important feature in striking or kicking for you to remember. In striking, for example, the rearmost foot is pressed hard against the ground and the resulting reaction force is passed through the body and arm to the striking hand; adding force to the punch. When the hand actually strikes the target, the shock of the blow is passed through the body to the feet of the striking individual to the floor and then recoils back the same path adding additional force to the blow. The principle is identical for kicks.

Breathing Control: It is well known that exhaling aids in contracting the muscles while inhaling tends to relax the muscles. This will find a most important and very direct application in your study of self-defense, where the breath is exhaled sharply from the diaphragm in the form of a yell during the execution of tactics of self-defense and inhaled after their completion to restore the oxygen content of your blood. A great deal more on breathing control later.

Psychological Principles

Since self-defense involves direct contact between two or more human beings, psychological factors play a very important role. Very often the psychologically stronger individual prevails even when outmatched physically. These principles will be learned in the course through the acquisition of competency in the physical skills combined with the development of control skills that will lead to the confidence and caution required to successfully defend yourself.

The major psychological concept we will deal with is embodied in the symbol of the mind like water. This concept is central to learning how to defend yourself.

This symbolism refers to the mental attitudes required while facing an actual opponent. Mind like water refers to the need to make the mind calm as a pond without any ripples on its surface. In this course we have used this symbol both in our meditation and in practice to achieve a state of mind like "a pond, in the middle of the forest, with no ripples." To carry the symbolism further, smooth water reflects accurately all objects within range, and if the mind is kept in this state, apprehension of the opponent's movements, both psychological and physical will be both immediate and accurate, and one's responses both defensive and/or offensive, will be appropriate and adequate. On the other hand, if the surface of the water is disturbed, the images it reflects will be distorted or, by analogy, if the mind is hysterical or preoccupied with thoughts of attack or defense, it will not apprehend the opponent's intentions, creating an undesirable condition.

An important psychological tactic in self-defense is eye contact. We focus our attention on the *eyes* of the assailant for three reasons:

1. To intimidate him. A clear, steady gaze directly into his eyes will unnerve the opponent.
2. To watch for "telegraphing." Only the most experienced fighters can avoid "telegraphing" (via looking at the spot to be attacked) his intentions. If you are able to predict and antici-

pate his next move, you are in a much better position to avoid or counter it, as the situation calls for.

3. To look, by your peripheral vision, for a route of escape. It is obviously to your advantage to avoid a perilous situation, but if you cannot, the physical tactics you will learn will allow you to repel the assault of your attacker long enough for you to escape quickly. If you want a skill-level to be able to go fifteen rounds with your assailant, go to a Karate school; plunk down your money, and plan to spend *at least* a year or two at it. But your best bet is to learn to yell and use your physical skills to avoid or escape your assailant's attack; and then to *RUN AWAY* as quickly as you can. Make up a story of what you did to him later.

Unity of Mind and Will: To use a modern analogy, if the mind is compared to the speaker of a telephone, the *will* is likened to an electric current. No matter how sensitive the speaker is, if there is no electric current, no communication takes place. Similarly, even if you anticipate the movements of your assailant correctly and are conscious of an opening on his physique, if the will to act on this knowledge is lacking, no effective defense can take place. The trained mind may find an opening, but the *will* must carry out the technique called for. This means you must be both able *and* willing to inflict pain on your assailant to protect yourself.

Combined Physical and Psychological Principles
Focus is the concentration of all the energy of

the body in an instant on a specific target. This involves not only concentration of physical strength, but also the type of mental concentration we have discussed above. This principle will come up frequently during your learning and practice experiences, so a clear understanding of it at this point is important. A defensive technique executed without *focus* is ineffective.

This part of our discussion is central to your study of self-defense, and without an understanding of it your learning will be so faulty as to be useless. We will discuss two major subject areas here: the nature of your assailant and the yell.

The Nature of Your Assailant: It is vitally important, to begin with, to distinguish between a "mugger" and a rapist. Realizing there are exceptions, the difference between the two is their ultimate intentions. Both will accost you; but the "mugger" is after your valuables; the rapist has as his goal sexual assault.

Give the "mugger" your purse, packages, etc There is nothing that is in them that cannot be replaced. It is also likely that the robber will be so quick or efficient that you will be unable to effectively resist, anyway.

The potential rapist is another matter entirely. To begin with he probably falls into one of two general categories: (1) he either knows you or has "seen you around," or, (2) he encountered you at random in an area and by a method with which he is familiar. In either case, he is *afraid* of you!

If he weren't he would have picked a much more acceptable way to meet you; few lasting friendships arise from such encounters.

It is imperative that you understand that it is fear or anxiety that causes him to assault you and not raw lust or the full moon. We will concentrate the *majority* of our energy in this course on capitalizing on this knowledge.

The Yell: Whichever category your assailant falls into you have a very powerful weapon to use against him. This weapon is noise. Noise in this course will be manifested in the fashion both most effective and the least likely to fail you: A YELL. Every technique we will learn and practice has this one element in common: a loud, clear, sharp yell that is forced from the center of your body by your diaphragm and focused on your assailant. This concept is *central* to your learning an effective defense system!

It should be clear by now that this yell is a *weapon*. You, your attacker and every other human being is born with, and will die with, two fears: the fear of loud noises and the fear of falling. To utilize these fears that he already has, combined with the greatly increased likelihood that your yell or yells will attract attention and enhance the probability of getting third-party assistance against the assailant makes its mastery very worthwhile.

It is a form of breath control which we have discussed above. That it be forced up from the center of your body and focused outward onto your

assailant by the use of your diaphragm and abdominal muscles is important, for a number of
reasons:

1. When you are tense or upset your throat becomes constricted and "dry"; in such condition it is a poor defensive tool. If, however,
   you are prepared and trained to use your diaphragm to execute your yell this problem will
   not arise.
2. As we discussed above, *exhaling* allows you
   to get greater efficiency from the muscles you
   are using to protect yourself.
3. When confronted with a potentially threatening
   situation your body will produce and inject
   into your bloodstream large amounts of adren-
   alin. The oxygen you breathe in after a loud,
   lung-clearing yell will act as a catalyst with this
   bodily stimulant and briefly give you more
   strength, better hearing and sight and more
   speed with which to RUN AWAY from your
   attacker.
4. Most important, it frightens your assailant;
   and may even make him run away. Remember,
   he is *already* afraid of you, he tends to be
   more timid than fierce, and your yell is very
   likely to attract attention and/or assistance,
   which would not suit your assailant's purposes.

We are most emphatic on this point. In a threatening situation the defensive tool most likely to
allow you to escape unharmed is a *loud yell*. We
know how effective a yell can be from statistical
studies: in one study, 60% of all assaults on
women that were successfully repelled were repelled all or in part by a loud, clear, sharp YELL!

Women who have either taken my classes or watched the T.V. series and have followed our advice of making lots of noise when confronted or when they suspect they are about to be confronted have reported uniform success in escaping attack; some of these have been against *armed* assailants, as well. Yell.

General Precautions: Some precautions you should take to avoid having to deal with an assault:

1. Have secure locks and peepholes on the door to your home or apartment.
2. Do not let strangers into your home. Utility personnel have identification with a picture on it. If you are still unsure, call the utility. He'll wait. If someone wants to use your telephone ask him for the number through the closed and locked door and call it for him.
3. Have the phone number of a friend or nearby neighbor as well as the number of the police permanently taped on your phone.
4. Never leave the keys in the obvious places outside. If you can find them, so can someone else.
5. Report suspicious strangers to the police. The police have told me repeatedly they don't mind; their job is to protect you. Help them do it.
6. Avoid poorly lighted areas.
7. Look before you get into your parked car. Day or night. Front and back seat. A great many women have been seriously injured or killed every year by not taking this simple precaution. If someone is in there, scream and run for help.

Always lock your car—no matter where you park it or for how long. It is a small inconvenience in light of the possible consequences.

8. If someone signals for assistance on the road drive to the nearest phone and tell the police. They will be able to help a stranded motorist or apprehend a dangerous person.

You know that most men are not very good fighters, and most such encounters are "won" by the best "bluffer." You can bluff by taking a firm, resolute stance and yelling, but if need be, punch or kick him and you will be the master of the situation. Too much timidity can be dangerous to you. While you argue with or talk to an aggressor he can maneuver you into a disadvantageous position. If you are unsure—challenge. If necessary—attack.

Remember, that in sixty percent of all assaults on women the loud noise, *by itself,* repelled an assault. Also remember that it can be a simple matter to avoid most dangerous situations by being alert, observant and keeping your distance. Never be afraid to kick off your shoes and run! Yell, if necessary. If anyone questions you for doing this tell them that a third degree black belt in Karate told you distance is the great equalizer.

MISCELLANEOUS MATTERS

If the course is given to women who have limited time to invest in a "class," twenty to thirty hours of *intensive* instruction with the student practicing on her own for fifteen to thirty minutes every day has, in our experience, sufficed. Obviously, the more time in instruction and practice the greater the likelihood of a better result.

As to clothing, the student can wear slacks, a sturdy blouse and tennis shoes rather than a *dobok* or *gi* (the traditional Karate and judo suits). No special clothing or equipment is needed, although the student needs *some* experience in striking solid objects. The reason for this is that the student's normal reaction is to "pull" a kick or blow on approaching a solid object (body). Such a reaction both slows and renders ineffective her tactic. To overcome this reaction and to allow the student to get the "feel" of "focusing" her blow or kick on a solid object, she should practice striking solid, yet not hard, surfaces.

There are conmmercial and "homemade" objects available to all. The commercial *Kwon-go* or *Makiwara* are essentially Karate punching bags made of canvas-covered hard rubber prisms on a solid backing. These are available from martial arts supply houses, costing from $4.00 to $20.00. The so-called "body bags" of canvas filled with cotton or sand are also usable. Some classes have used gymnastic or "tumbling" mats hung on a wall. Some more enterprising students have tied heavy pillows to posts, raising or lowering them for kicking or punching. The object of the punch, blow, block or kick is irrelevant as long as it gives the person striking it the opportunity to throw a full-force blow into a solid surface without hurting herself. This practice should be repeated often enough to get the student beyond the "pull" reaction, and to the point that she can regularly deliver full-force focused blows while maintaining her balance.

The class can be conducted both indoors and outdoors. Indoors, mats on the floor are required to avoid injury. Outdoors, grass is normally sufficiently resilient to allow safe practicing. When practicing outdoors avoid allowing bypassers to gather and watch. It distracts the class and often makes them nervous and self-conscious, and the bystanders cannot learn anything of use by a few minutes' casual attention.

Warm-up exercises of the calisthentic sort that loosen tight muscles, making them supple and limber are the ones that should be chosen at first. The sequence of warm-up exercises is up to you. After a time include in each set of warm-up exercises, done in unison, basic punch, snap kick, elbow blows, all three blocks as well as anything else desired by the student or instructor.

Every practice and class session should begin not only with warm-up exercises, but begin *and* end with two or three minutes of group meditation. The instructor should train the group in mastering the symbol of the mind like water. We choose to concentrate our mental energy on the image of "a pond, in the middle of a forest, with no ripples." Considerable effort can justifiably be invested in this endeavor.

In the back of this manual you will find a "Striking Chart." It presents a front and a rear view of the male anatomy, and is accompanied by a key to the effects of blows to various parts of the body. Students must become very familiar with it. A random blow, or one aimed at a target not maximally susceptible to attack, will not serve her well. But an effective blow delivered to a susceptible target may save her life.

STUDENTS SHOULD REREAD THIS SECTION AS OFTEN AS IS NECESSARY UNTIL THEY UNDERSTAND IT. WITHOUT AN UNDERSTANDING OF THE ABOVE THEY WILL BE POORLY EQUIPPED TO DEFEND THEMSELVES.

LESSON I
Preliminary matters

MEDITATION

Begin by taking a comfortable position, kneeling, clearing your mind of the day's matters, and then attempting to focus the energy of the mind on the mind like water symbolism of "a pond, in the middle of a forest, with no ripples." Exhale slowly and deeply; then inhale in the same way. Repeat. When mastered, this concept of controlled physical and mental energy is known as "dhayana" in yoga, "chan" in Chinese and Korean religions and "Zen" in Japan.

WARM-UP EXERCISES

Do those calisthenics that loosen and strengthen the body. Jogging may be included.

THE BASIC STANCES

The two stances we will learn in this course are the "Horse" Stance and the "T" Stance. Each has its own purposes, advantages and disadvantages, which we will discuss as we learn them. Most important, however, is that you be aware that a firm, well-balanced stance is both a more formidable image to an assailant who, after all, expected *no* response from you (or he would have let you alone) and a more effective position for self-defense. Give these stances the practice they deserve. All the defensive tactics and techniques are executed from them.

"Horse" Stance

Your feet should be pointed *straight ahead* as opposed to their normal angled position and should be shoulder-width apart. The ankles should be flexible to allow you maximum ability to respond either by running away or by a given tactic or technique.

The knees require special attention here, as well as in all other tactics in the course. Our earlier discussion related that the most effective techniques are those executed from the *center* of your body, using your abdominal and hip muscles. Keeping a "spring" in your knees of necessity forces you to begin your response with those muscles. "Spring" means a *moderately* tensed bounce; knees slightly "knock-kneed" (keep your feet pointing straight ahead for greater balance) and bent. This may seem slightly uncomfortable at first, but experience and practice will overcome this. You will use your buttocks and hips for balance as a counterweight to compensate for and add to the effectiveness of your responses.

The back should be erect for two reasons: one, for purposes of observation of your situation and, two, to utilize your back, hip and abdominal muscles as a "springboard" to add to the effectiveness of your response. Likewise, the head should be erect and your eyes alert and observing, focused on the eyes of your assailant.

Horse" Stance (Front)   *"Horse" Stance (Side)*

Positioning of your arms is simple, but requires the same care and attention to detail that the other tactics do. The fists are clenched; placed on your hipbones, palms up. The shoulders are erect, and "set" but *not* tensed. Your elbows are pulled towards each other at the rear as though there were a strong rubber band between them. This is to allow you to punch either frontward, upward or rearward without wasting your kinetic force in useless arcs that only minimize the effectiveness of your response.

The total picture of the "Horse" stance, then, is as though you are astride a horse, gripping its sides with your knees.

This stance is most useful against attacks from the rear, as well as in attacks with more than one assailant in front of you. Your eyes are alert for routes of escape and for other potential attackers.

"T" Stance

This stance is to defend yourself against frontal and lateral assaults. The physics of equal distribution of weight across your feet, keeping "spring" in your knees and the "springboard" back, remain the same as in the "Horse" stance.

"T" Stance (Front)

Your feet should be at right angles to one another; the rearmost foot pointed *away* from your body and the forward foot pointing straight ahead. Remember to keep the weight evenly distributed across your feet and the "spring" in your knees.

Your hips should be flexible to allow for the quickest response to a rushing attack. You should jump aside rather than taking a rushing assault head-on, if you can!

Depending on which leg is forward (right or left) the opposite hand should be clenched and resting lightly on the hipbone, palm up, ready for response. The other arm and hand should be extended over the foreward leg, palm *down* to block. It should be three to four inches above the thigh—any higher would give an assailant a tempting "handle."

Eye contact is particularly important here as you are *facing* your attacker. Remember, steady, confident eye contact (1) *intimidates;* (2) allows you to watch for *telegraphing;* (3) allows you to look *peripherally* for a route of escape.

PRACTICE

From a normal stance practice snapping into one, then the other, stance. When "setting" into the stance give a loud, clear, sharp yell *from the diaphragm.* Repeat this until you can quickly assume a well-balanced "Horse" or "T" stance that will allow you to execute the quickest, most effective escape or response.

With regard to the "T" stance as well as all other tactics, *do not* become over-reliant on either side of the body. Don't always have the left (or right) leg extended. Practice punches, kicks, blocks, etc., with both sides, so you develop no "weak" side that is more vulnerable to attack.

TECHNIQUE

Specific techniques for the "Horse" stance will come later, but the "Following Defense" is a good beginning skill to acquire.

The student should walk six to eight feet in front of someone acting as a potential assailant, who is walking at this separation behind her. When the student chooses, she should quickly and firmly turn to face her follower, take a well-balanced "T" stance (this is a *frontal* assault), yell on getting "set," look him directly in the eye and wait for the situation to be clarified, then respond appropriately.

The student will find that the physical and yelling responses will upset and unnerve the "assailant" for reasons discussed in the preceding chapter, in the section on principles of Karate.

This is a good tactic to execute if you are being followed, or think you are and prefer *knowing* to to fear and doubt. It is a *very* effective tactic to turn to face an assailant and give a loud yell from the diaphragm.

In an actual situation *do not* talk to such a person; there is a great deal of experience telling us this is a favorite tactic of rapists to "talk" you into a perilous situation. Make him declare himself. You will be astounded how often he will merely run away.

FALLS

Before we begin our next technique you must learn how to fall safely. This is important to you for two reasons; first, it will enable you to practice without injuring one another, and second, it will teach you how to fall without being injured and to get up quickly if an assailant manages to knock you down.

We will cover one basic fall briefly. It can be learned quickly, and with little effort.

The "back fall" is merely sitting down and allowing the buttocks to tuck themselves "under" so as to avoid the shock to your spine of your entire body weight. Then you roll onto your back, absorbing the force of the fall. The arms should be semirigid and extended full length to the sides at shoulder level. As the body rolls onto the back while falling backwards, the arms and hands should *vigorously* slap the mat to absorb as much force as is possible.

Note: The chin should be *firmly* held on the breastbone *throughout* the course of the fall to avoid injury. *Remember this!*

*Back Fall
(Standing, arms
extended)*

*Back Fall
(Rolling through)*

Practice this fall until you are able to fall quickly and get up running or into the stance called for by the hypothetical situation you are defending against.

MOVING TAKEDOWNS

These two tactics are designed to meet the contingency of an attacker grabbing at you at the shoulder, chest or neck level.

Remember: "do not meet a wave head-on," absorb his forward inertia, turn into it and use it to your advantage and against him. When you meet his onrushing force be angled in relation to him, to avoid "meeting the wave head-on" and to be able to turn his force against him (see photo).

Both tactics are executed from the "T" stance since it is assumed you are *facing* your assailant. Remember the principles of balance and alertness. The "spring" in your knees will allow you to respond quickly and to absorb some of his forward inertia so that you will not be overcome by it and lose your balance.

Straight-Across Takedown

The straight-across takedown is used against an assailant who is facing you and throwing a blow toward you at shoulder level either with his right or left fist. Since this maneuver is difficult to visualize at first, be sure to refer to the illustrations. First, as always with a frontal assault, assume a well-balanced "T" stance. As the assailant's fist comes toward you, use a short upward block to deflect the blow away from your body. Then in the same motion, firmly grasp his wrist and twist it so that his palm faces *away* from you. While you are twisting his wrist, turn your body so that the shoulder of your free arm is up against his chest.

Straight-Across Takedown
(Meeting the blow)

Quickly thrust your free arm under his armpit and *firmly* trap the upper part of his arm in the crook of your arm with a vise-like motion. Draw his upper arm toward your chest for a secure grip. A

Straight-Across Takedown
(Countering and arm lock)

Straight-Across Takedown
(Down and arm locked)

this point the arm with which he tried to strike you is secured at his shoulder and wrist. Press his lower arm away from you to "lock" his elbow by his wrist.

Any joint will bend if moved in one direction, but it will break if sufficiently forced in the other direction. This anatomical fact makes *any* bodily joint vulnerable. With concentrated practice you can block the blow and get a firm double grip on the assailant's arm quickly and smoothly before he realizes what is happening. Then by bending the arm back, you are able to apply however much painful pressure on his arm is needed to prevent the attacker from using his free arm against you. With his arm now braced across your chest and "locked," place the leg closest to him firmly behind his leg in order to trip him backwards. Turn your torso in the direction that will cause his body to fall *away* from you. This twist of your torso should be executed as soon as you are settled against his torso and have secured his arm. The twist, however, should not cause you to lose your balance; if you are not well-balanced, correct your position or your stance, as required.

The twist will throw your attacker to the ground. Now you have countered his assault and should either flee immediately or "lock" his arm at the elbow joint by inserting the knee closest to the arm against the back of his arm between his elbow and armpit. Pressure is applied by bending your knee slightly forward. Very little forward pressure will break his arm at the elbow joint. Be careful in practice.

Cross-Body Takedown

This tactic is to counter the shoulder-level blow or grab aimed at you, but delivered *across* your body (right to right or vice versa). It, too, is executed from a "T" stance.

Cross-Body Takedown (Countering)

The incoming blow or grab is countered by using your blocking arm to push his arm *away* from your body *but* in the *same* direction it is already traveling. This will allow you to utilize his forward inertia against him.

Next, grab the wrist (or thereabouts) of the arm you just blocked, and strike him with your other clenched fist just *above* (i.e.: towards his body) his elbow on the back of his arm with a "closed-fist blow" (see below, this lesson). This blow is very painful as well as giving you the leverage on his arm to throw him onto the ground. Then RUN AWAY!

Cross-Body Takedown (Striking)

At the point you blocked his arm, and when you struck his upper arm, a loud *yell* is called for. This will frighten and disorient him, giving you time to react or escape.

Learn the movements of these techniques slowly until you understand what you are doing, then add the yells, and then execute them more quickly until you are able to handle a full-speed attack. Remember, do *not* become over-reliant on either a right or left side of your body. Develop the ability to work from either side equally.

PUNCHES AND BLOWS

Basic Punch

This is one of the basic weapons in your self-defense "arsenal." It should be practiced until perfected. *Every* lesson and practice session should include 50-100 repetitions of the basic punch.

Begin by clenching your hand into a tight, hard fist. When you strike someone your first two knuckles contact the struck surface, the wrist must be kept straight and "locked," and at the point of contact, the elbow should "lock" as well.

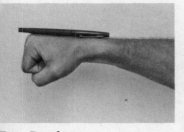

Basic Punch

The "straight and locked" wrist is important to you because if the hand is either bent back or down from your arm the blow will be ineffective and painful—to you! To understand a "straight and locked" wrist, hold first one arm; then the other, in front of you at eye level, palm down across your body so you have a clear side view of your wrist and hand. Lay a pencil along your wrist to the back of your hand and move your hand until little or no light shows between the pencil and your hand. To be "locked" means the wrist will keep itself straight and will not bend. To achieve this effect begin with a "straight" wrist, tense the muscles of your forearm until your wrist won't give much when you attempt to manipulate it. Practice this with *both* arms, first one, and then the other. You must be able to punch with either arm equally well.

Basic Punch

From "T" stance the first punch is delivered by the rearmost arm, with the "blocking" arm going backward to the hipbone as the first punch is delivered. A punch is *returned* as quickly and with as much vigor as it is *delivered* because this allows the force of the returning punch to be conserved, recoil from your feet and be returned to your attacker with your next punch. The second and consecutive punches should find the fists crossing in midair, wasting no energy that can be applied to an attacker.

The punch then begins on the hipbone, palm upward, and is projected in a straight line forward to the body of the assailant. The blow began in the stomach and hips and is delivered, in this case, by the fist. As the fist, palm upwards, begins to cause your arm to straighten, as it travels forward it is to be turned over, palm down locking the arm into a stiff, straight weapon with the elbow joint "locked" and the fist in contact with the target. This is a smooth motion. Hip, straight line, turn hand over, lock arm as you strike. The arm remains extended for a moment to allow your focused energy to travel into the opponent's body. Resist the temptation to become a "punching machine." One effective blow delivered to a susceptible target is much more effective than many unfocused blows on random targets.

You should begin as soon as possible to practice striking solid objects such as the ones mentioned above. Also, be alert to rotation or "reaching" to get to a target. If he is out of reach use another tactic or step closer to him. "Reaching" only causes you to lose your balance.

Knife-Hand Blow

You may recognize this as the "Karate" or "judo" chop. I'm sorry to tell you that MGM has gotten greater results with less effort than you will.

The wrist, again, as in *all* blows must be straight and locked. The elbow and arm will also be straight and locked at extension as before.

The blow is delivered as a "chop" by a downward sweep to a susceptible target (such as the base of the neck or a collar bone) with the meaty edge of the palm as the striking surface. It may also be used to "jab" by extending the arm forward in a straight line, using the tips of the fingers to strike with. It is delivered in this fashion exactly as a basic punch would be to such targets as the throat or solar plexus. *Yell* on contact.

Knife-Hand Blow

Extended Knuckle Blow

This blow also utilizes the straight and locked wrist and elbow principles, but its delivery is done downward and by the motion of a snake striking at a prey (i.e.: in a slight arc).

The striking surface is indicated in the photo and the targets for this non-vicious tactic are the back of your opponent's hand or the front thigh muscles. It can be quickly used in either of the stances or in a seated position, and is thus useful in those "difficult," as well as in more dangerous, situations. Practice it from both stances and a seated position. As always, no blow is effective unless it is quickly and accurately delivered to a specific target and is *focused.*

Extended Knuckle Blow

Closed-Fist Striking

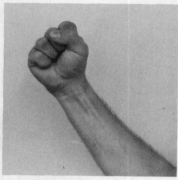

Closed-Fist Blow

Here, refer back to the comments on Knife-Hand Blows since all that was said there applies here. The only difference between the two is that many students have expressed more confidence in the efficacy of this blow over the knife-hand. It is merely the basic punch with the striking surface being the butt of the palm rather than the knuckles. It is used on many targets and in many techniques such as the Cross-Body Takedown. *YELL* as you hit him!

MEDITATION

Close each lesson as you began it by learning the power of your mind and how to control it. Use the "pond in the middle of a forest" to pacify your mind, to evaluate how your body has reacted to the lesson. This will also prepare you to return to other activities on a lower level of energy output.

You can use this symbolism to allow you to calm your mind so you can eliminate conflicting mental images and focus your latent energy.

Very briefly, you will feel this energy more as you develop, but it will begin as a deep feeling of well-being and strength. In this course we will expose you sufficiently to this concept to train you to remain calm during a threatening situation. To get further into this concept you may want to embark on a study of yoga or a deeper study of one of the martial arts.

LESSON II
Standing your ground

MEDITATION

Begin with a period of meditation, such as was first discussed in Lesson I, page 23.

WARM-UP EXERCISES

Do those calisthenics that loosen and strengthen the body. Jogging may be included.

REVIEW

Stances

You should be able to run down a checklist of the components of the "Horse" stance and the "T" stance, and should begin your warm-up exercises from one or the other of them. The stances should be firm, steady and well-balanced by now if you have practiced them outside the class.

Checklist for stances:

1. Feet well balanced with weight evenly distributed along their bottom surfaces. Feet positioned according to the stance in question.
2. "Spring" in the knees; knees slightly bent. In

"Horse" stance the knees should be slightly "knocked," as well.

3. Hips "loose" to allow you to swing away from a leaping attack or into one that cannot be avoided so as to be able to use its force against the attacker.

4. Back erect to give greater observing ability and to act as a "springboard" for your punches.

5. Head erect. Steady eye contact.

6. Arms positioned in regard to the blocking or striking requirements of the appropriate stance. Wrists *straight and locked.*

Basic Punch, Closed-Fist Striking, Straight-Across Takedown

With all the above tactics, you should now, as a matter of course, *yell* not only when you "set" into your stance, but upon striking the selected target. *Always* yell when you strike or kick. It makes your tactic much more effective than it would be without the yell.

SNAP KICK

The snap kick is also basic to successful self-defense. It should be included in *each* practice session, and at a minimum in class as part of the warm-up. You should practice this against a solid surface to achieve strength, accuracy and speed as well. Also, be alert to becoming over-reliant on either leg as your "best" one. Practice with *both* for the best defense, and if one is less effective work on it to make it as strong as it could be. Do not forget that in this, as in all else we will learn, your *yell* upon making contact with the target you have chosen will greatly add to its effectiveness and thus to protecting you.

Snap Kick from "Horse" Stance

Snap Kick from "Horse" Stance (Knee up)

Snap Kick from "Horse" Stance (Leg at extension)

From "Horse" stance you are best prepared for an attack from the rear, so why snap kick? The reason is that more than one person might assault you, and some of them might be so positioned as to be vulnerable to a kick or punch.

To execute a snap kick from the "Horse" stance, begin in a steady, well-balanced stance, draw knee and foot to a position approximately in front of your navel, draw your knee *at least* as high as your navel, curl your toes back toward your body, and kick the *lower* part of that leg and foot at whatever target you choose using the ball of the foot to strike the target. *Yell!* The lower leg should swing freely. Don't slow your kick by tensing your muscles. Your buttocks should be tucked "under" to whatever degree required to keep you in balance. Return the leg to its place; then repeat with the other leg. This kick, as all blows, should begin with and be driven by the abdominal and hip muscles. This is a strong, quick defensive tactic; improve it by using *all* your strength.

It is vital that you have your knee high enough, that the leg swings freely, and that you *focus* your blow on a *chosen* (not a random) target. Acquire equal skill with both legs. The kick is an excellent tactic to practice in front of a mirror as it allows you to see what is happening while you are doing it. It may be helpful to practice as many of the tactics and techniques as are feasible in front of a full-length mirror, if one is available.

Snap Kick from "T" Stance

The kick from this stance is nearly identical to the above, except that by virtue of the positioning of your feet in "T" stance, certain movements are different.

For practice purposes let the first kick be from the rearmost leg. Draw it forward until it is under your navel and slightly in front of it. Draw your knee sharply upwards until it is at least navel-high. Then, as before, thrust the foot and lower leg to the target swiftly and strongly. Curl back the toes using the ball of your foot to strike your target, so as not to injure your toes. After this delivery, return your leg to its original position.

Snap Kick from "T" Stance (Knee up)

Snap Kick from "T" Stance (Leg at extension)

To kick with the forward leg, draw it upwards, with the knee at navel-level and kick as above. Yell on contact with your target.

In practice alternate which leg is forward so as not to become over-reliant on either side of your body.

FOOT STAMP

This simple tactic can be used either when your assailant is close behind you or when he is in front of you.

Simply draw your knee upward as in the snap kick, except that you concentrate your force on thrusting your foot downward, heel first, onto the top of your attacker's foot. If you miss the first time, try again until you get the desired result. Remember your yell. When he has released you or stepped back from you, RUN AWAY.

PUNCHES AND BLOWS

Use this time to perfect your aim, focus and coordination.

KNEE-TO-GROIN

When your opponent is facing you, and has drawn you, face first, against his body, this is one of the few times that the groin is a good target. Normally, his reflexes would be faster than your attack against the groin.

If possible, take a "T" stance, and as in the snap kick, draw your knee sharply upward into his groin. Yell. The foot remaining on the ground should be pressed as hard as you can against the ground while your striking leg moves upward as quickly as possible into his groin. Practice this with both legs.

After successfully delivering this blow push your assailant to the ground and RUN AWAY.

HAIR TAKEDOWN

There are three variations to this technique, but all share some common characteristics.

1. They are all executed from "T" stance.
2. Their object is to use the pain of the opponent's hair being pulled to get him down.
3. In all three his head should be drawn back or to the side to throw the assailant off-balance.
4. They all must be executed quickly and with a loud yell.

Front Hair Takedown

From "T" stance, step up quickly to your assailant, grab his hair at the front of his scalp *firmly* between your fingers, thrusting your arm straight backward so as to cause his head and neck to bend backward, yell, and take another quick step

Front Hair Takedown

Side Hair Takedown

forward to throw him off-balance and to the ground and then RUN AWAY.

Side Hair Takedown

Executed as above except that you are either at your assailant's side or move to his side because he is too tall to do a Front Hair Takedown on, and you grab the hair on the *side* of his head, pulling him over and down while yelling and then RUN AWAY.

Rear Hair Takedown

Again, as in the two above takedowns speed, accuracy and a loud yell are essential. In this tactic we assume your attacker is turned *away* from you, perhaps he has grabbed your purse and is running away with it.

Rear Hair Takedown

Rear Hair Takedown

From a well-balanced "T" stance grab the hair on the *back* of his head, drawing it back and throwing him to the ground by his hair. Get moving.

MEDITATION

Close each lesson as you began it with a period of meditation, as discussed on page 36.

LESSON III
Close-in defenses

MEDITATION

Begin with a period of meditation, such as was first discussed in Lesson I, page 23.

WARM-UP EXERCISES

The warm-up at this point should include at a minimum your choice of calisthenics, jogging, basic punch, snap kick and all possible tactics should be executed from both "Horse" and "T" stances.

REVIEW

Review the Cross-Body Takedown, Knife-Hand and Extended Knuckle Blows and Hair Takedowns.

STRAIGHT-ARM DEFENSE

This tactic is quite similar to the basic punch. It is performed against someone in front of you, who is blocking your way. This is a good tactic to use if you are in a small, enclosed area, such as a doorway, and want out.

Straight-Arm Defense

The straight-arm defense is executed much as a basic punch from "T" stance, but instead of punching your assailant you strike him with your fist on the outer edge of his shoulder as though punching (yell) while pressing down on your feet for maximum force.

The object is to turn his torso sufficiently to let you zip by and escape. Don't underestimate the utility of a loud, lusty yell in such a situation.

COLLAR GRAB WITH KNEE-TO-GROIN

Collar Grab with Knee-to-Groin

In Lesson II we covered knee-to-groin; this tactic is performed in the same rigorous fashion, from "T" stance and with a loud yell, except that here we assume his legs are sufficiently spread to allow a knee to enter between them, but he has *not* pulled you close enough to attack this target.

Quickly move close enough to grab the collar of his shirt, grasp it firmly with both hands and simultaneously draw your knee (either one) into his groin as discussed in knee-to-groin. Yell on contact with your target, and as soon as possible push him to the ground and ESCAPE.

COLLAR GRAB CHOKE-HOLD

From "T" stance grab one side of his collar with one hand, quickly crossing the other over it to grab the other collar. Rest the back of your hands

Collar Grab Choke-Hold

against his Adam's Apple, pressing backward for choking pressure and to cause him to lose his balance. Kick him in the shin or knee and push him to the ground. RUN AWAY.

MEDITATION

Close each lesson as you began it with a period of meditation, as discussed on page 36.

LESSON IV
Taking the advantage

MEDITATION

Begin with a period of meditation, such as was first discussed in Lesson I, page 23.

WARM-UP EXERCISES

Do those calisthenics that loosen and strengthen the body. Jogging may be included.

REVIEW

Review the Collar Grab Choke-Hold and Knee-to-Groin.

WHERE AND HOW TO STRIKE

At this point and before each lesson and practice session for the duration of the course familiarize yourself with the Striking Chart at the end of the book.

No tactic, no matter how well executed, will have its maximum potential effect unless it is delivered to a susceptible target. A random blow to the head cannot have the effect of a well executed punch to the solar plexus. But, to strike the solar plexus you must first know where it is, what will happen if you hit it, and *then* move against it.

The striking chart in the back of the book indicates the various consequences of blows to different targets.

Basic Punch to Solar Plexus

Snap Kick to Shin

Some targets for you to consider, and suggested ways to attack them are:

1. Basic Punch to Solar Plexus
2. Snap Kick to Shin
3. Closed-Fist Strike to Collarbone
4. Basic Punch to Thigh
5. Snap Kick to Side of Knee
6. Knife-Hand Chop to Adam's Apple.

All such blows must be delivered quickly and with their force focused. A loud, clear yell should accompany each blow on contact with your target. You will see that the combinations of both single

Closed-Fist Strike to Collarbone

Basic Punch to Thigh

Snap Kick to Side of Knee

Knife-Hand Chop to Adam's Apple

and multiple blows and kicks against all the available targets is very effective indeed. You should begin to work out some combinations of these on your own from now on.

ADVANCED PUNCHES AND BLOWS

Eagle's Claw

This blow is delivered with the same technique as the basic punch. The wrist must be "straight" and "locked"; the elbow must be "locked" at extension of the arm when it strikes the target and the blow must be delivered with speed and focus. Yell on contact with your target.

Its distinctive characteristics are the configuration of the fingers and Eagle's Claw's target.

The fingers are spread apart as far as they will go, and are *bowed* as in the illustration. The fingers are *rigid* so as to provide you with a supple weapon against your assailant. Practice with both hands until you are comfortable with your fingers deployed in this way.

Eagle's Claw

Your target is your opponent's *eyes.* Most students are hesitant to move against such a target because they fear doing permanent damage to him. My answer to this is twofold: one, *he* attacked you, and is likely to do you serious harm and indignity unless stopped, and two, it is unlikely that you will develop sufficient *speed of striking* in this course to have your blow contact his naked eye. What is more likely is that you will lacerate his eyelids and frighten him! Also, the psychological impact of the combination of this type of blow and your simultaneous yell should be *very* obvious to you at this point and should encourage you to reread the section on yells and practice them with even greater purpose.

If your assailant is wearing glasses, the blow is delivered in basically the same way. But, instead of jabbing your fingers directly into his eyes, bring them first into contact with his cheekbones at a point immediately below the frames of the glasses and continue your full-force blow *under* the glasses and on into his eyes; yell.

The Eagle's Claw is potentially very dangerous, and you should avoid practicing it, or the next tactic, in the presence of children. Their imitative nature requires that you use your best judgment.

Finger Jab

Finger Jab

This tactic is executed like the above and the basic punch. In this tactic you use a rigid, extended index finger as your primary weapon instead of your knuckles, palm or all of your fingers.

It may be used much like the Eagle's Claw against the eyes, but may also be used against the hollow of the throat, solar plexus or lower abdomen.

This tactic, like all others, must begin in the abdominal and hip muscles. The force is then transferred to the arms for delivery.

Short Upward Elbow Blow

Short Upward Elbow Blow

This blow is struck using your elbow as the striking surface. It is a very powerful blow and is used against an opponent facing you at close range and is aimed at such targets as the solar plexus, ribs, and under the chin depending on the target available to you in a given situation.

From "T" stance, strike upwards, *leading with your elbow* until your fist is beside your ear. The blow must be delivered with both speed and force and accompanied by a yell.

The fist, then, has traveled in an arc either from your hip or the front of your thigh, depending on which arm delivers the blow. If you deliver the blow with the "blocking" arm, it will be necessary to turn your fist palm upward as you begin to strike so as to minimize the muscular resistance from your own body as you deliver the blow. This is a simple accommodation that will insure an effective delivery by *either* arm.

Rearward Elbow Blow

The Rearward Elbow Blow is delivered from the "Horse" Stance since it is assumed that your opponent is close behind you or has grabbed you from behind. All the principles of focus, yells and balance apply here as in all other tactics, but you needn't *choose* your target. In this tactic and from your position relative to your attacker virtually any such blow will meet with a susceptible target on his torso.

The first move is to draw either of your fists from the hipbone and quickly bring it, palm towards your body, three or four inches in front of the breast on the side of your body *opposite* its beginning point (i.e.: right fist over left breast or vice versa). From this "cocked" position immediately return the arm, *elbow leading,* back to its position on the hipbone, palm up. It is this "return trip" from your breast to hipbone that constitutes the blow, and this is where you should accelerate your arm, elbow first, to strike your opponent's torso.

*Rearward Elbow Blow
(Fist up to chest)*

Practice with both arms to avoid over-reliance on either one and remember to press your feet firmly on the ground, use your knees to "flex" the power of the blow into your assailant and to yell.

Rearward Elbow Blow (Striking)

This technique may also be used to free yourself if grabbed from the rear. The power of your repeated (and alternated, left-right-left, etc.) blows will loosen his grip and allow you to escape. A Foot Stamp might also be useful in such a situation to free or help free yourself.

Both the Short Upward Elbow Blow and the Rearward Elbow Blow must become a regular part of your self-defense studies from now on. Each lesson and each practice session should include them in *at least the Warm-Up Exercises.* These are two very valuable weapons in your growing self-defense arsenal. By study and conscientious practice develop them to the point that can best protect you.

THE PURSE ARSENAL

This brief discussion is designed to "break the ice" for a discussion in the class on the subject of weapons other than the body of the student herself that may be used in self-defense.

As for pistols and knives we discourage our students from even possessing them for the following reasons:

1. The possible legal complications arising from unlicensed or illegal possession of a deadly weapon.
2. The high possibility of an accident involving either herself or innocent third persons.
3. The practical liabilities of the speed with which

one can bring the weapon into play to defend herself.

4. The probability of the lack of skill with the weapon and/or reluctance to use it, making a dangerous situation *worse* and perhaps giving an otherwise unarmed assailant a weapon.

For these reasons we discourage our students from displacing their alertness and developing false courage with a weapon. Also, you can't *drop* your hand.

As to the rest of the purse arsenal, it is only useful if you have sufficient time to bring it into play, and this would be controlled more by the situation than the will.

One tactic universally accepted is to buy a "police whistle" at a hardware or sporting goods store for 98¢ and put it on your keyring. By carrying the keyring in your hand, you have handy a mechanical substitute for your yell. And, as discussed above, in one exhaustive study done on assaults of all kinds on women, in 60% of the cases of successfully repelled assaults a loud, sharp noise, *by itself,* repelled the assault! This has also been borne out in the experiences of our students, and we commend it to you highly.

Students and instructors in our classes have also come up with the following suggestions.

The Purse Arsenal (Credit card)

A credit card held in the palm, gripped by the thumb and middle finger and braced by the index finger used to slash at the face and throat of an attacker.

The Purse Arsenal
(Spray can to eyes)

A spray can of *anything* (*caution:* some chemical sprays such as MACE and the like are prohibited by law to the general public in many states) will irritate the eyes, and breathing function of an assailant due to their freon and alcohol content if sprayed in the eyes or face.

A comb can be held in the hand much in the manner described for a credit card (above), using the teeth of the comb to scratch and lacerate the face and throat of an assailant.

In all of the above uses of weapons the principles of balance, choosing your target and yelling loudly apply as in any other tactic.

MEDITATION

The Purse Arsenal
(Comb to face)

Close each lesson as you began it with a period of meditation, as discussed on page 36.

LESSON V
The quick response

MEDITATION

Begin with a period of meditation, such as was first discussed in Lesson I, page 23.

WARM-UP EXERCISES

Do those calisthenics that loosen and strengthen the body. Jogging may be included.

REVIEW

Review the Short Upward Elbow Blow, Rearward Elbow Blow, Snap Kick and Straight-Across Takedown.

BLOCKS

All the blocks have this in common:

1. They are executed from the appropriate, well balanced stance and are accompanied by a yell on contact with the blow or kick to be blocked.
2. Since their purpose is to block a blow, stab or kick, they must be executed quickly in order to deflect the incoming blow, etc. before it strikes you.

Short Upward Block

*Short Upward Block
(Starting from "T" stance)*

Normally done from "T" stance the "blocking" arm sweeps in an arc from its position 3-4 inches above the front of the thigh, across the chest, at whatever height called for, to stop the incoming blow; meeting it with a yell and sufficient force to deflect the threat.

You should practice this, as all else, with *both* arms until you acquire sufficient proficiency to protect yourself from this sort of attack in all situations. If you are struck it will reduce your ability to respond, so avoid it, if possible. If it is *not* possible to avoid being struck, recover as quickly as you are able, so as to continue your defense and foil the attack on you.

To give this tactic sufficient force to deflect the blow you should pay particular attention to having a firm, well-balanced stance, pressing your feet to the ground, and beginning the response from those strong abdominal and hip muscles.

Also, remember *eye contact:*

1. to *intimidate* your assailant
2. to watch him for *telegraphing*
3. to look (peripherally) for a route of escape.

*Short Upward Block
(Blocking action)*

After you have blocked the blow you may choose to do a takedown, punch or kick him with whatever combinations you might choose, or take this opportunity to RUN AWAY, if possible.

All of this discussion applies to the blocks we are about to learn, as well.

Short Downward Block

This block is used against a kick thrust at you from the front, or perhaps against an animal (such as a dog) you wish to escape. It may be executed from either a "Horse" or "T" stance, as can the other blocks described here, as the situation requires.

*Short Downward Block
(Starting from "Horse" stance)*

The block begins with the hand and fist in the downward position, over the thigh in "T" stance, and 3-4 inches in front of your groin in "Horse" stance. Sweep whichever arm you are using for this block in an arc across your chest to a position three to four inches in front of your *opposite* breast; immediately return the arm in a reverse of the operation just completed with sufficient speed and force to stop or deflect the blow coming at you; yell on contact.

If he loses his balance, you can either attack him in response, or push him to the ground and escape.

*Short Downward Block
(Blocking action)*

Double Upward Block

This block is to protect your head and upper torso from an attack with a stick, club or knife. It is important that you are balanced, calm and leave a good opening between your arms in the extended (upward) position to allow you to observe your assailant and look for a route of escape.

Double Upward Block
(Hands crossed at groin)

Double Upward Block
(Hands at chest)

Remember, rather than meeting a blow head-on, you are better served to jump aside or take as little of the blow as you can. This applies here, as well as everywhere else in the course.

From "T" stance, quickly position your arms, palms towards your body, crossed in front of your groin. Next, lift your fists to chest height so that your left fist is over your right breast and vice versa, palms toward your body. Then *thrust* them straight upwards, turning the fists *away* from the body as they cross the eyes, and lock your arms, elbows *slightly* bent (see illustrations) at extension. Be sure there is a "window" between your arms so that you can observe your opponent and anticipate and counter his next move before it can harm you. You *did* yell, didn't you?

At first, this block sounds unnecessarily complex, but as you can see it is composed of only three

Double Upward Block
(At extension)

basic components: fists crossed over groin, drawn upward to the chest with the palms turned toward the body, then *thrust* the fists and arms upward, turning the palms *away* from the body as they cross the eyes, and lock the arms, fists crossed, elbows slightly bent at extension to ward off potentially dangerous blows or stabs.

Some students ask why this "complicated" method? The alternative methods are too *slow* because the muscles of your body resist upward movements. Try some. This method allows the quickest, surest response to such attacks. Practice will overcome your initial problems with this or any other tactic.

After this block has been executed you might feel unable to react *offensively* toward your assailant. Not so! You have your kicks to use against him.

Kick Block

Kick Block

This block is designed to protect your groin area against kicks. Take a "T" stance, then *thrust* your arms downward and cross them in front of your groin, palms toward your body, as in step #1 of Double Upward Block above. This barrier of crossed fists and arms, if firm, will stop or deflect the main force of such a kick.

After you have blocked his kick he will be off-balance. Act quickly to push him to the ground (grab his leg and *twist!*) or counterattack with whatever tactics are appropriate to the situation and then RUN.

WRIST GRAB DEFENSE

Wrist Grab Defense

This tactic is used if someone in front of, or perhaps seated beside you, grabs your wrist. From a "T" stance (or, if seated, from a steady, firm pressing against the chair or seat with your body and firmly against the floor with your feet) execute a swift Short Upward Block. This will put so much pressure on his thumb as to force him either to let go or have his thumb broken. Yell! After having broken his grip either escape or move immediately into your next tactic, as the situation requires.

ARM AND WRIST LOCK #1

This tactic is executed if someone grabs your wrist, forearm or purse, his left arm grabbing your right or vice-versa.

From "T" stance, quickly execute a short downward block with the arm grabbed. Yell! Step into the gap between his arm and body, swinging the appropriate (right or left) leg behind his leg, planting it firmly behind him, with the back of your knee against the back of his knee. This will provide you with a solid "post" to trip him over with the closed fist blow you deliver to his shoulder socket as your foot settles behind him, back of knee to back of knee, as described above.

By simultaneously positioning your leg behind his and striking him, you utilize your accelerating body mass as it is drawn to the ground, while your hip and abdominal muscles, as well as your closed fist blow to his shoulder socket will cause him to collapse backward over your leg. All this, in sum, when mastered, will allow you to escape your attacker unharmed!

Arm and Wrist Lock #1
(Short downward block)

Arm and Wrist Lock #1
(Back of knee and striking)

Arm and Wrist Lock #1
(Assailant down, arm locked)

ARM AND WRIST LOCK #2

Also executed from "T" stance, this tactic is simpler to perform, and assumes your assailant has reached *across* your body while facing you to grab at your wrist, forearm, purse or hand-held object.

When the assailant reaches *across* your body and grabs your wrist, execute *quickly* a short upward block with sufficient force to keep him moving in the direction he was moving with his grab. Then turn your body in the opposite direction of his movement, stepping *behind* him as he passes

Arm and Wrist Lock #2
(Short upward block)

Arm and Wrist Lock #2
(Striking)

and execute a closed-fist blow onto his upper arm two to three inches *above* (i.e.: towards his torso) his elbow. Yell! If properly executed this will throw your attacker forward and to the ground, allowing you to step around him and escape.

If you are unable to execute the closed-fist blow to his upper arm as described above, choose an alternate punching or kicking target, such as the kidneys, ribs, side or back of knees, to knock him *away* from you and allow you to escape. If any of these alternatives becomes necessary, remember *how* to strike, and how your yell adds to the effectiveness of your tactics.

MEDITATION

Close each lesson as you began it with a period of meditation, as discussed on page 36.

LESSON VI
Countering the attack

MEDITATION

> At this point you should be able to *see* the "pond in the middle of a forest, with no ripples," and transfer this metal state to your defensive tactics for a greater defense ability.

WARM-UP EXERCISES

> Along with your jogging and calisthenics at this point you should be including, *at a minimum,* 50 reptitions *each* of basic punch, snap kick, short upward block and short downward block, all executed from *both* stances.

REVIEW

> Review the Arm & Wrist Lock #1, Collar Grab Choke-hold, Hair Takedowns (Front Hair Takedown, Side Hair Takedown, and Rear Hair Takedown) and Falls.

REAR TRIP THROW

> This tactic is designed to free you from an attacker who has grabbed you from behind, and is attempting to pull you over backwards with his arms around your neck and throat.

Rear Trip Throw is executed from the "Horse" stance, and it is imperative that you have a firmly set, well-balanced stance and have retained the "spring" in your knees. You will find that the greater the separation between your feet, the closer to the ground you will be and thus better able to execute this throw. If you find that throwing your assailant causes you great exertion, re-examine your execution of the throw after re-reading the instructions. Remember, any effective tactic must use the strong abdominal and hip muscles of the extremities which are faster, but weaker.

When grabbed, as described above, go immediately into a *low* as possible "Horse" stance. This may choke you slightly, but will start *him* bending forward, and begin the forward inertia needed to execute this tactic.

Rear Trip Throw
(Breaking away from choke)

Upon "settling-in" to your stance, immediately thrust your buttocks and hips backward into his mid-section with as much speed and vigor as you can manage. *Yell!* This will do two things: (1) prevent you from being pulled over backwards by your assailant, and (2) continue the forward inertia needed that was begun as you executed your stance.

Rear Trip Throw
(Grabbing arm)

At the same time that you thrust your buttocks sharply into his body, grab whichever arm he has grabbed your throat with that is *on top* and draw it down and away from your throat to act as a *lever* as in the illustration. "Lock" the elbow joint as in other tactics. You will probably find that if you thrust your buttocks backward resolutely enough your stronger abdominal and hip muscles will break the grip of his weaker arm muscles. If not, use your fingernails or repeated applications of the above to break his grip. Insert the thumb of your other hand into the armpit of his other arm and press it in *hard* against the pressure point there. This will assist you in lifting his weight from your back, and with his other arm as a lever allow you to control the direction of his fall.

The next step is simple, but sometimes students have difficulty with it. Turn your torso quickly and resolutely, leading with the shoulder under the arm you are using as a "lever" on your opponent's body. You now "drop" the knee on the *opposite* side of your body to allow him to roll off your back, tripping him by his knee-joint, which is now "locked" as it is braced against the back of your thigh. If you do not try to "carry" him on your back and if you remember that to avoid this you must "lead" with the proper shoulder and "drop" your knee, you will now find your opponent on the ground, immediately in front of you, and you still have a firm grip on the arm you were using as a lever. If he had not been twisted to the ground by your strongly turning torso his knee joint would have broken due to its "locked" position behind your thigh. Likewise, now that he is on the ground, move the appropriate knee in to "lock" his elbow joint by placing it between his elbow and shoulder and bending your knee forward bringing your hip muscles into play to secure the elbow joint.

At this point you may choose to escape, break his

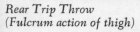

Rear Trip Throw
(Fulcrum action of thigh)

Rear Trip Throw
(Assailant down, arm locked)

arm by adding more knee-pressure to his locked elbow joint, or punch or kick him. The choice is yours, but remember *escape* is your ultimate goal.

TWIST THROW

Twist Throw
(Arms around torso)

This tactic is to counter the same situation as above except that either you have been grabbed around the *torso* immobilizing your arms rather than the throat *or* you were, for some reason unable to break the grip of the arms in the above assault. It is executed in much the same fashion as the Rear Trip Throw, except that since you are unable to grab his arms you must execute this technique without having one of his arms to act as a lever. The back of your thigh is still your fulcrum, and the buttocks must be quickly and resolutely thrust back as before, and the shoulder "leading" and knee "drop" are the same, but in this technique you will have no arm to "lock" when he is on the ground. So, you must be prepared to punch or kick him *quickly,* if you so choose, so that you can escape.

In *both* of these throws you must first learn the components of the throw, executing them slowly until you know and understand them well enough to begin to execute them with greater speed and effect.

Twist Throw

PUSHING DEFENSE

The pushing defense is to offset someone pushing with one or both hands against your chest

Pushing Defense
(Clasping hands to chest)

Pushing Defense
(Bending forward)

Pushing Defense
(Twisting opponent to ground)

either to annoy you or to push you over. The response is simple and effective; the only difference between being pushed by one or both of your opponent's hands is whether or not you place *both* of your hands over his (a single-handed push) or only *one* hand on each (a double-handed push).

When the push gets to your chest (assuming you weren't able to block it) clasp one or both of your hands *over* the hand or hands pushing you and *press them* (or it) *firmly* to your chest and quickly and firmly bend forward from the waist. The holding of his hands will immobilize them, and your bending forward will "lock" his wrist joint(s) at a right angle (90°) and render him helpless with pain. If he attempts to stand or pull away he will sprain or break his wrist(s).

From your bent-over position turn your body so as to "lock" his elbow joint, as well, and thrust him to the ground. The direction required to "lock" the elbow will depend on which arm you are attempting to "lock" if it is a *single*-handed push, but *either* direction (right or left) will work if it is a double-handed push. Practice this technique against all three possibilities until you can execute them all smoothly and quickly. Yell when you clasp his hands to your chest. Once he's down, what to do next is, once again, your option.

MEDITATION

Close each lesson as you began it with a period of meditation, as discussed on page 36.

LESSON VII
Protecting the body

MEDITATION

Begin with a period of meditation, such as was first discussed in Lesson I, page 23.

WARM-UP EXERCISES

Do those calisthenics that loosen and strengthen the body. Jogging may be included.

REVIEW

Review the Rear Trip Throw, Twist Throw, Striking Chart, Blocks (Short Upward Block, Short Downward Block, Double Upward Block and Kick Block) and Wrist-Grab Defense.

Hand-Pressure Arm Lock
(Grabbing assailant's hand)

HAND-PRESSURE ARM LOCK

In this technique, executed from "T" stance, instead of your assailant grabbing you on the hand, wrist, forearm or purse, *you grab him* on the hand. This might be useful as a defense against a purse-snatch attempt or knife attack. Again, let us remind you there is *little* likelihood your assailant will be armed, but preparation for such an unlikely eventuality can only *help* you.

Hand-Pressure Arm Lock
(Thrusting hand back)

Hand-Pressure Arm Lock
(Striking back of elbow)

Hand-Pressure Arm Lock
Shoulder under opponent's arm)

This technique assumes that you are able to intercept your assailant's hand, grabbing him so that your palm covers the back of his hand. Note also, that you are grabbing him *cross-body.* Upon grabbing his hand yell loudly and, using your abdominal and hip muscles as well as your arm, thrust his hand back at him, directly toward and as close as possible to his nose. At this point strike him *hard* with a closed-fist blow two or three inches above the back of the elbow joint to continue his turning away from you. Yell on striking. As his back is now towards you continue pressing his hand and arm upward, and slide your shoulder under that arm. Grab his other arm or shirtsleeve to secure him in your armlock.

Once he is "locked," and your shoulder is firmly planted under this "locked" arm, you then must decide whether to break his arm or to push him to the ground to escape. If he is armed, we suggest that you break the arm by pressing sharply upward with your shoulder. This is because he has proved himself deadly and thus must be incapacitated as quickly as possible for your safety.

In practice, remember that it is very easy to harm your practice partner, and such an event would neither help you learn self-defense nor encourage partners to work with you. Be careful.

1. At the point you thrust his hand at his face you "lock" the wrist joint. Go slowly.
2. At the point you strike his upper arm (and yell) you cause pain. In practice sessions use only enough force to overcome any resistance to being turned around.

3. When you place your shoulder under the arm to be "locked" there is a danger of breaking the arm at the shoulder joint. Use only enough upward pressure to secure the arm and get the "feel" of "locking" his arm in this fashion.

DOUBLE WRIST-GRAB DEFENSE

Double Wrist-Grab Defense
(Breaking loose)

Done from "T" stance, this technique is used to break free when someone has grabbed *both* your wrists or hands from in front of you.

Simply execute *two* Short Upward Blocks at the same time. When the pressure from the blocks breaks his grip, you then have your hands free to aid in your defense. Yell when you execute the blocks—it gives you additional strength and will frighten and confuse your attacker.

In this situation, your feet and knees are free even though your hands are temporarily immobilized. You might execute kicks to shins, knees, thighs or abdomen; knee-to-groin or any combination of the above to add to the effectiveness of this technique.

CHOKE-HOLD BREAKING

Front Choke-Hold Break

Again, exercise caution in class and practice sessions to avoid injury to yourself or your classmates when learning and mastering these Choke-Hold Breaks.

From "T" stance execute a Double Upward Block

Front Choke-Hold Break
(Down to block)

Front Choke-Hold Break
(Breaking)

Front Choke-Hold Break
(Punch to solar plexus)

to break the grip on your throat. Yell when striking his inner forearms. Use your abdominal and hip muscles for the requisite strength.

Once his grip has been broken, quickly use a closed-fist blow to his collar bone. The arm *not* used for this blow should simultaneously be returned to the appropriate hipbone; then a basic punch should be executed to his solar plexus. Yell! During the time this basic punch was being delivered the fist that struck the collarbone before should be returned sharply to *its* hipbone in preparation for its immediate use to deliver a basic punch to his Adam's Apple. Yell!

Front Choke-Hold Break
(Punch to Adam's Apple)

After this response the student should immediately and alertly resume her "T" stance, watching his eyes, in case further blows or kicks are required. It is unlikely, however, since the blow to the collarbone should immobilize the arm on that side of his body, the punch to solar plexus will interrupt breathing and heart action, and the punch to his Adam's Apple will precipitate further breathing difficulty and nausea. For these reasons exercise caution in practice and vigor in self-defense.

Rear Choke-Hold Break
(Grabbing fingers)

Rear Choke-Hold Break
(Arms at extension)

Rear Choke-Hold Break
(Throwing to ground)

Rear Choke-Hold Break

This technique assumes you are being choked around the neck from the rear by an assailant's hands. From "Horse" stance grab his *little* (or "pinkie") fingers *firmly* in your hands as in the illustration. Quickly and firmly extend your arms, at shoulder level, as far outward as they will go. This will so "lock" these fingers as to render your assailant literally helpless with pain. Almost *any* resistance will break one or both of these fingers so practice with care! Now thrust your buttocks back as in the throws and, using his arms ("ducking under" the arm crossing over as in the illustration) throw him to the ground. He is drawn across the back of your thigh and his knee is "locked" in the same manner as in Rear Trip Throw and Twist Throw.

Once he's on the ground release his arms, kick him in the ribs and run away.

MEDITATION

Close each lesson as you began it with a period of meditation, as discussed on page 36.

LESSON VIII
General review

REVIEW

At this point in the course both the instructor and the student should be aware of those techniques in the course that should be given special attention and practice. Work on these, and any others desired, until the student is proficient in all the skills in the course.

POSTSCRIPT

We have come to the end of our course; yet it is a mere beginning. You must continue to practice and meditate to retain your skills. An hour or two on a weekend, for example, will provide you with moderate but healthful exercise while maintaining your proficiency in your self-defense skills.

Please re-read Part I of this text as often as required until you understand it. This should take some time. We all seek understanding. Remind yourself of the importance of avoiding conflict, as well as the value of being able to control it, if necessary. Practice with care, remember your yells, learn "focus," and be alert to dangerous situations so as to *avoid* them.

Key to diagrams

The letters indicate striking areas. The numbers indicate the degree of pain resulting from blows to the area.

1. moderate pain
2. sharp pain
3. stunning and/or numbing
4. temporary paralysis or unconsciousness
5. severe injury, possibly permanent injury or fatality. This degree of retaliation is justified only in the face of a vicious attack in which your life is threatened seriously.

Key to front view

		LIGHT BLOW	MEDIUM BLOW	HEAVY BLOW
A	temple	3	4	5
B	nose	2	3	4
C	ear	1	2	
D	under jaw	1	2	
E	neck muscle	1	2	
F	side of neck	2	3	
G	wind pipe (Adam's apple)	3	4	5
H	shoulder muscle	1	2	
I	hollow of throat	3	4	
J	solar plexus	2	3	
K	side, under last rib	1	2	
L	lower abdomen	2	4	
M	elbow joint, inside	1	2	
N	forearm	1	2	
O	wrist	1	2	
P	back of hand	1	2	
Q	fingers	1	2	
R	upper and lower thigh	1	2	
S	knee	2	3	
T	shin	2	3	4
U	ankle	1	2	
V	instep	1	2	
W	groin	3	5	
X	eyes	5	5	

Key to back view

		LIGHT BLOW	MEDIUM BLOW	HEAVY BLOW
A	base of skull	3	4	
B	center of neck	2	3	
C	seventh vertebra, base of neck	3	4	
D	back, center, between shoulder blades	2	3	
E	kidneys	3	4	
F	back of arm	1	2	
G	back of elbow joint	1	2	
H	back of upper leg	1	2	
I	back of knee	1	2	
J	calf	1	2	
K	tendon, Achilles' heel	1	2